A Christian Understanding of the JEWISH FESTIVALS

Hanukkah - Passover - Rosh Hashana

Yom Kippur. - Sukkot (Tabernacles) - Purim

Tisha B'Av - Shavuot - Yom Yerushalayim

Yom HaShoah (Holocaust Remembrance Day)

Copyright © 2020 Edward DeVries
ISBN: 9798583018000

Published by
www.bibleschol.edu

Introduction

In the Old Testament, God gave His people days of feasting and celebration. He gave them as days of remembrance. Many of our modern-day Jewish holidays are those same days of remembrance that we read of in the Bible.

The Christian faith is deeply rooted in the Old Testament tradition. Jesus and His Apostles were practicing Jews who faithfully observed all of the days of feast and celebration that we now know as Jewish holidays. As they observed the holidays, Jesus and His Apostles were intimately familiar with their symbols, and with their significance (both historical and spiritual). The same cannot be said for many if not most of our Lord's modern-day followers.

Should Christians Celebrate Jewish Holidays?

The short answer is no. The Bible places no requirement upon Christians to celebrate Jewish holidays. There is, however, a beauty, a richness, and a historical and spiritual understanding that comes from them. As Christians, while we are not bound to Judaism, we do well to at least understand and respect the traditions that Our Lord Himself observed.

Table of Contents:

Hanukkah

"And it was at Jerusalem the feast of the dedication, and it was winter."

-- John 10:22

We will start with Hanukkah, sometimes spelled Chanukah, as it is perhaps the best-known Jewish holiday.

The name "Hanukkah" derives from the Hebrew verb חנך, meaning "to dedicate." Hence, in John 10:22, the celebration of Hanukkah was translated as "the feast of the dedication."

Hanukkah is the story of God's provision for His people and represents His continued presence in the most trying of circumstances.

Established as the balance of world power shifted from the East to the West when Alexander the Great conquered the known world, Hanukkah began is during the rime in between the Old and New testaments. 175 years before the birth of the Christ-child, Judah found itself under the harsh tyranny of Greek ruler Antiochus Epiphanes, who desecrated Temple in Jerusalem and converted it into a pagan temple for idols.

With his desecration of the Temple and the harsh treatment of the Jewish people, Jewish forces led by Judah Maccabee led a rebellion against the Greeks and drove them from Jerusalem in 164 BC. When rededicating the temple to the worship of God, there was only enough oil left to light the Temple's candelabrum for one day. Yet that single days' worth of oil burned for eight days, and this miracle became what we now know as a festival celebrating the victory of light over darkness.

In spite of its popularity, Hanukkah is a minor holiday when compared to the others in this book. But because of its proximity to Christmas the symbols of the menorah and of children playing with the dreidel have become familiar Holiday sights and made the "Festival of Lights" a major part of the "Holiday Season" for Jew and Gentile alike.

Passover

"Now the first day of the feast of unleavened bread the disciples came to Jesus, saying unto him, Where wilt thou that we prepare for thee to eat the passover?"

-- Matthew 26:17

Each time you have observed the Lord's Supper (Communion) at your church, you have celebrated a portion of the Passover meal.

While the Christians' observe occurs at many times, and at any time, throughout the year, for Jews, the whole meal, or "seder," is more complex and happens only once a year.

The word "seder" means order, which is appropriate because the meal is very ordered and very structured. Because of this structure, the meal has remained the same for thousands of years.

The Passover observance, which always happens in the Spring, recalls the exodus from Egypt. It revisits the miraculous acts of God that finally convinced Pharaoh to 'let the people go,' freeing Israel from slavery.

During the Passover, no leaven (yeast) is eaten, and the house undergoes a ceremonial cleaning. The fact that this important celebration takes place in the home mirrors the very first Passover, when the Hebrew people remained in their homes as God worked out his final plague in Egypt: "For I will pass through the land of Egypt this night, and will smite all the firstborn in the land of Egypt, both man and beast; and against all the gods of Egypt I will execute judgment: I am the LORD. And the blood shall be to you for a token upon the houses where ye are: and when I see the blood, I will pass over you, and the plague shall not be upon you to destroy you, when I smite the land of Egypt. And this day shall be unto you for a memorial; and ye shall keep it a feast to the LORD throughout your generations; ye shall keep it a feast by an ordinance forever" (Exodus 12:12-14).

Among the important symbols are the four cups. The Cup of Sanctification, The Cup of Deliverance, The Cup of Redemption and The Cup of Praise. At the seder meal, four cups of wine will be consumed by the adults. Each cup has a special significance.

The cup we drink when we take the Lord's Supper is the third cup, the Cup of Redemption. Here is how we see it in the Gospels, "And he took the cup, and gave thanks, and gave it to them, saying, Drink ye all of it; For this is my blood of the new testament, which is shed for many for the remission of sins. But I say unto you, I will not drink henceforth of this fruit of the vine, until that day when I drink it new with you in my Father's kingdom. And when they had sung an hymn, they went out into the mount of Olives" (Matthew 26:27-30).

Jesus is the fulfillment of the third cup. The fourth cup, He is yet to drink, the Cup of Praise. He leaves this cup as the promise of His return and of the restoration of all things.

Of course, keep in mind that from the Jewish perspective Jesus is not the Messiah. Therefore these cups do not point to Him. A practicing Jew would reject and resent these applications.

Rosh Hashana

"Create in me a clean heart, O God; and renew a right spirit within me."

--Psalm 51:10

While many of us consider January 1st to be the New Year, the Jewish New Year, called Rosh Hashana, is celebrated in the early Fall.

This is also considered to be the day that Adam and Eve were created in the garden and humans began their time on earth.

According to the Jewish calendar, the current year (2020) is 5781. That means that Adam and Eve were created 5781 years ago.

The standard greeting on Rosh Hashana is, "L'shana Tova" which translates roughly as "good year." It is a prayer for the year ahead. Each year the Jewish people pray to be granted another year and to be "created" clean again, just as Adam and Eve were created clean and free from sin.

Rosh Hashana is both a day of judgment, and a day of hope for what is to come.

While the decision for "another year of life" is handed down on Rosh Hashana, the verdict is not "sealed" until Yom Kippur. Therefore, the 10 days from Rosh Hashana to Yom Kippur are a crucial period when most peoples' judgment "hangs in the balance."

Yom Kippur, 10 days after Rosh Hashana, is a solemn and important day.

Yom Kippur

-- Leviticus 23:27

Yom Kippur, often called the Day of Atonement, is the holiest day for the Jewish people. It is observed by a 24-hour fast which begins just before sundown (when the Jewish day begins) and lasts until the following sundown.

Historically, the day begins in the Sinai desert with Moses coming down from the mountain to find the people dancing around the golden calf. God's man pleads with God to forgive the people of this horrible sin.

It was on Yom Kippur when Moses brought the second set of tablets down from the mountain, representing "a clean slate" and a day of forgiveness for God's people (Exodus 20).

While another year of life is granted on Rosh Hashana, the verdict is "sealed" on Yom Kippur.

Sukkot

"And the LORD spake unto Moses, saying, Speak unto the children of Israel, saying, The fifteenth day of this seventh month shall be the feast of tabernacles for seven days unto the LORD. On the first day shall be an holy convocation: ye shall do no servile work therein. Seven days ye shall offer an offering made by fire unto the LORD: on the eighth day shall be an holy convocation unto you; and ye shall offer an offering made by fire unto the LORD: it is a solemn assembly; and ye shall do no servile work therein."

-- Leviticus 23:33-36

Five days after Yom Kippur, the Feast of Sukkot, also known as the "Feast of Tabernacles, is another remembrance of the Exodus, and of God's deliverance from Egypt.

It is a time of great joy, celebrating that God has granted a new year, and that He continues to provide for His people.

It is also a festival of harvest and provision from God and is a week-long celebration.

During this holiday, Jews build "sukkots" which are a booth or tent-like structure. So some refer to the holiday as the Feast of Booths. These small structures commemorate the temporary structures Israelites lived in while wondering in the wilderness during the Exodus.

Purim

"For if thou altogether holdest thy peace at this time, then shall there enlargement and deliverance arise to the Jews from another place; but thou and thy father's house shall be destroyed: and who knoweth whether thou art come to the kingdom for such a time as this?

-- Esther 4:14

Throughout history of Israel, there have always been those who would seek to destroy God's people. Yet God continues to sustain and deliver. Purim is the celebration of yet another one of these times of deliverance.

Read the book of Esther, which records the events leading up to this deliverance.

At the time of the Feast of Purim, observant Jews read the Book of Esther and each mention of the name of Haman, the man who plotted the Jews' destructions, is read it is a custom to hiss or make a noise mocking him.

The day ends with a festive meal, celebrating the people Haman sought to eliminate.

Tisha B'Av

"And in the fifth month, on the seventh day of the month, which is the nineteenth year of king Nebuchadnezzar king of Babylon, came Nebuzaradan, captain of the guard, a servant of the king of Babylon, unto Jerusalem: And he burnt the house of the LORD, and the king's house, and all the houses of Jerusalem, and every great man's house burnt he with fire."

-- 2 Kings 25:8-9

In contrast with the joy of Hanukkah and Purim, this major feast is a mournful, solemn period in Jewish life.

Lasting for three weeks, this observance represents a time the Jewish history when the most calamity had fallen upon the "chosen" people.

This period is also referred to as the period "within the straits", found in Lamentations 1:3, which reads, " *all her persecutors overtook her between the straits.*

The observance begins on the 17th of Tammuz and ends on Tisha B'Av (the 9th day of the month of Av). These days always fall within the summer months on our Gregorian calendar.

During these three weeks, no celebrations are held and there is no music. Observant Jews also abstain from things like haircuts, or weddings.

It was on Tisha B'Av, that the following tragedies have occurred in Jewish history:

> During the time of Moses, the Jews accepted the slanderous report of the 12 Spies, and the decree was

issued forbidding the children of Israel from entering the Promised Land (1312 BC).

The First Temple was destroyed by the Babylonians and Nebuchadnezzar (586 BC).

The Second Temple was destroyed by the Romans (70 AD).

The Jewish Bar Kochba revolt was defeated by the Roman Emperor Hadrian. The Temple Mount was plowed under, and Jerusalem was rebuilt as a pagan city. (135 AD).

The banishment of all Jewish people from England by King Edward (1290).

The expulsion of Jews from Spain (1492).

The outbreak of World War I (1914)

The mass deportation of Jews from the Warsaw Ghetto (1942).

All of these are observed during three week's of mourning, remembrance, and of sorrow for the calamities that have befallen the Jewish people throughout history.

Shavuot

"And when the day of Pentecost was fully come, they were all with one accord in one place. And suddenly there came a sound from heaven as of a rushing mighty wind, and it filled all the house where they were sitting. And there appeared unto them cloven tongues like as of fire, and it sat upon each of them. And they were all filled with the Holy Ghost, and began to speak with other tongues, as the Spirit gave them utterance."

-- Acts 2:1-4

Celebrated on the 50th day after the Passover, Shavout commemorates Moses receiving the law on Mt. Sinai.

The name "Feast of Weeks" comes from the seven weeks between this day and Passover (7 days of 7 weeks equals 49 days).

The Greek word for this holiday is Pentecost, which means 50, and this is the name that is more familiar to Christians.

During Shavuot, Jews read the Ten Commandments to commemorate the giving of the Law to Moses. Additionally, some Jewish people may decorate their homes with flowers, and drink milk, as the Jewish people received the Law as newborn children.

The New Testament significance of the holiday is in that this is the holiday when the disciples were gathered in Jerusalem and received the Holy Spirit.

To the Christian, this event is the follow up to the Passover promise of Christ: as He fulfilled the promise of the third cup, this is God replacing ceremonial and sacramental laws with a new Law that would dwell within us through His Spirit.

Of course, this interpretation would be rejected by Jews.

Yom Yerushalayim

"How shall we sing the LORD'S song in a strange land? If I forget thee, O Jerusalem, let my right hand forget her cunning. If I do not remember thee, let my tongue cleave to the roof of my mouth; if I prefer not Jerusalem above my chief joy."

-- Psalm 137:4-6

Jerusalem, the city where King David established his kingdom and where Solomon built the Temple, ceased to be Israel's capital when the Roman army attacked and destroyed much of Jerusalem in 70 A.D. Yom Yerushalayim, or Jerusalem Day, celebrates the reunification of the city of Jerusalem, as the capital of Israel under Israeli sovereignty in 1967.

Yom HaShoah

A Prayer of the afflicted, when he is overwhelmed, and poureth out his complaint before the LORD. Hear my prayer, O LORD, and let my cry come unto thee... By reason of the voice of my groaning my bones cleave to my skin."

-- Psalm 102:1,5

Otherwise known as Holocaust Remembrance Day, this holiday is observed each year on January 27.

The Holocaust is often referred to as the "Shoah" which is the Hebrew word meaning "catastrophe."

The rallying cry on this day is "never again

The day is observed by lighting candles, often 6 candles for the 6 million who suffered in the concentration camps.

Conclusion

There is a rich tradition in each of these Jewish holidays.

Perhaps as you have read, you may have realized that as Christians, we are observing some of them, without even realizing it!

THE ABC's OF SALVATION

ADMIT:

Admit that you are a sinner and have made mistakes.

BELIEVE:

Believe that Jesus is God's only Son and He chose to die on a cross for you.

COMMIT:

Commit yourself to a life of following Jesus and serving others.